FABRIC PRINTING

Gisela Hein

FABRIC PRINTING

B. T. Batsford Ltd London

JM

First English Language Edition 1972
Printed in Great Britain by
The Anchor Press Ltd, Tiptree, Essex
and bound by Wm Brendon and Son Ltd, Tiptree, Essex
for the publishers B. T. Batsford Ltd
4 Fitzhardinge Street, London W.1
© Otto Maier Verlag, Ravensburg, 1971
ISBN 0 7134 2382 X

Contents

Introduction

The technique for printing on fabric is simple and easy to understand: colour is put on a pattern block with a roller or directly from an inking pad, then cloth is stamped with the inked block to transfer the pattern. This process is repeated at will. A design appears, an ornamental arrangement, a rhythmical progression. Technique and form alternate in relation to one another.

We attain insights when we go forward boldly. As we sort out our working materials we assimilate experience, develop technical and pictorial ideas, and feel our way to a personal form of expression.

A printed fabric fulfils an aesthetic function, in addition to its utilitarian purpose. This function should be in harmony with its practical requirements and many problems will present themselves here. If we want to master them we must be familiar with the principles of fabric printing.

Working Materials

The materials are cloth and colouring agents. (Cloth is also termed 'goods'.) The tool is a stamp or block.

Block is the general term for the tool we use to print a repeated pattern, that is, a unit regularly and, in theory, limitlessly repeated. In order to print the largest possible area with the block, one generally makes it a size that will permit it to be grasped in either one hand or both hands. This will reduce the labour for long lengths of cloth. Apart from this, goods of prescribed width should be printed without haste, therefore the size of the block is determined by the width of the cloth. Blocks are also referred to as stamps.

A stamp may be any manageable object that has a patterned or unpatterned printing surface, even a finger or hand. Its printing surface is not bound by any preconceived idea.

The word 'stamp', which comes from the verb 'to stamp', indicates the type of activity. Stamps and blocks are employed in relief printing. Their printing forms are worked out with the pattern raised, in relief form; material surrounding the pattern is removed and the surfaces left untouched are printed (as opposed to photogravure printing in which engraved lines and surfaces print, a method which is being widely adopted by the textile industry).

Since the cloth is patterned by direct printing, it is coloured in patches. This manner of colouration is only successful if the dye fulfils the following requirements: it must not run into the cloth and it must cling well to the block when transferred. Binding agents, or thickening materials, are therefore added to the dye; their water-absorbent qualities counteract the capillary action of the textile fibres. In addition to this they possess adhesive power, which fixes the pigments on the cloth. The thickening agents effect the one-side patterning characteristic of fabric printing, as they prevent a complete absorption of the dye solution. Only on fine goods, such as batiste and lamp-shade silk, when the pressure is strong enough, does the dye penetrate and print the complete pattern on the reverse side.

Working materials being limited to block, colour and cloth, the scope for design seems, at first, to be narrow. During the printing, however, manifold relations emerge between form and colour, between the forms themselves, and of printed to unprinted, that is, negative to positive, areas. When we begin, the technical simplicity of the craft conceals this richness. We perceive it with astonishment when we see the coloured shapes against one another on the cloth.

Work Process

The repetition of the printing process characterizes the technical procedure: we place one imprint beside the other. Out of the repeat of the same shapes a pattern arises. It indicates a coherent arrangement. Row-formation, symmetry, or axial distribution determine it in general.

Furthermore, the texture of fabric influences the intentions of the design. The right-angled arrangement of warp and weft indicates directions, which we note in printing. The fabric repeat itself suggests that this arrangement should be expressed in the simple repetition of shapes. The repeat is a manner of printing appropriate to the fabric.

Next, there is fabric printing that departs from the regularity of the repeat, or that has a pictorial character because it operates in a self-contained manner. Such arrangements are also orientated on the texture. They may be recapitulated as a whole and become a repeat.

A repeat demands mechanization and rationalization. Both are possible to only a limited extent in hand printing. They can, however, lead us to technical considerations and experiments. In this connection we also seek a design that will be right for the fabric. We only succeed in this if we develop the printing pattern from the nature of the working materials and the working fabrics.

For this reason it is important that we print on cloth from the beginning. In this way we learn the basic requirements of fabric printing and can, from then on, test and judge new printing techniques and unfamiliar working materials on their suitability for fabric printing.

Technical Instructions

Colour

We use hand-printing colours and permanent colours for fabric printing. These chemically pro-duced colours are wash-proof and weather-proof. The permanent colours become boil-fast if the printed fabric is ironed at the prescribed heat after drying. A printed fabric should not be sub-jected to cleaning; present-day chemical cleaning treatment would attack and decompose the colours.

The variety of dye is chosen according to the purposes of its use. Paste hand-printing colours lend themselves to printing with wooden, metal, and ceramic stamps or blocks. They are rolled out carefully on a glass or stone plate, about two roller revolutions in length, and then transferred by the roller onto the printing block. The colour should be slightly tacky in leaving the roller and the plate. An even amount taken up guarantees an equally even imprint, and the pasty con-sistency allows blotch shapes. The colours dry hard, but this disappears after several washings. The stiffness of the colour is less noticeable on decorative fabrics for curtains, covers, cushions, and so on, than on a clothing fabric. In either case the fabric falls better if we choose fine linear or dotted printing patterns. For thinning colours that have become too thick, and for cleaning the printing equipment and hands, turpentine substitute is used.

Permanent dyes are liquid, therefore the block must absorb some of the colour. Potato, cork, and felt stamps are suitable for this. The colour can be taken up directly from the glass plate, from a piece of felt saturated with dye (an inking pad), or it can be applied with a brush. Thinning and cleaning are done with water.

Permanent dyes come in transparent and in opaque colours. They may be applied thinly, leaving the fabric supple, and for this reason we prefer these colours to hand-printing colours for shawls, ties, kerchiefs, and other clothing fabrics.

It is desirable to use only a few basic colours; these can be mixed to obtain many graduations. We discover the contrast of bright and dull colours, of clear and sombre shades. Opposites may be softened and balanced in tonal value. The counter-play of colours and shapes can be employed to support the rhythmic arrangement of the overall design.

Fabric

We favour fabrics with a smooth, close surface, that is, cloths like net, cotton-bast, linen, batiste, and other types of cotton, as well as smooth-finish raw silks and lamp-shade silk. In the case of very fine cloth the weave is less decisive; the twill weave of a tie silk, for example (Figures 18*a*, *b*), proves just as suitable for printing as a linen weave. For first experiments inexpensive net is recommended.

Many fabrics are dressed, or sized, that is, prepared with stiffening starches and weighting minerals such as plaster, kaolin, etc., to give them a favourable appearance for sale. This dressing is temporary; it can be washed out. Before printing, the fabric should be desized by boiling it in a solution of soda in water and rinsing thoroughly, otherwise the colour, which lies on the dressing, will be rinsed out with it on first washing.

Silk is not dressed. Cotton-bast is dressed only a little.

Block

Many materials are suitable for making the block. One selects according to the use planned for it. For larger projects, wood, often in conjunction with metal, is preferred because of its resilience. A block is set with strong pressure, the larger the block surface is, the more strengthening it needs. Fist or hammer blows may be required.

The block should be of manageable size, so that it can be safely placed and removed without slipping on the fabric. Small stamps are provided with a handle. The size and shape of the stamp surfaces may suggest pictorial ideas. Technical and designing purposes determine the shape of the block. Simple shapes lend themselves to manifold arrangements. In the case of a block that is in itself rich in motifs, the printing design is, to a large extent, fixed. From this arise the two different ways of working: 1 The design can be discovered during the work. The printing process is flexible. 2 Formal and technical considerations are concentrated on the printing surface of the block. In this method the manner of printing is fixed; the shape is reproduced in the repeat.

In the course of work

A smock or apron should be worn. The work room floor should be covered with newspaper. Tools and materials should be distributed where they can be clearly seen and readily grasped, that is, colours and equipment are generally placed to the right of the fabric. The latter must lie smoothly; it is best stretched with thumbtacks on strong cardboard, wooden board, or on a wooden table-top.

The pad underneath should give a little, so that, above all, the pasty dye can be pressed more deeply into the fibres of the fabric. Foam material about $\frac{1}{4}$ in. thick covered with a layer of news-paper is sufficient for this. For printing with ink, newspaper will be enough.

Spots of dye on the equipment and hands can be unintentionally transferred to the fabric!

After printing, the equipment is cleaned; only the dried colour is difficult to remove. Residues of colour should not be kept; scrape them off the glass plate. Cleaning is easier if, instead of using a glass plate, we stretch household metal foil or wax paper on a board (fastened down with adhesive strips) and throw it away after use. Cleansing the equipment, inking pads included, of water-soluble dyes is done simply under running water.

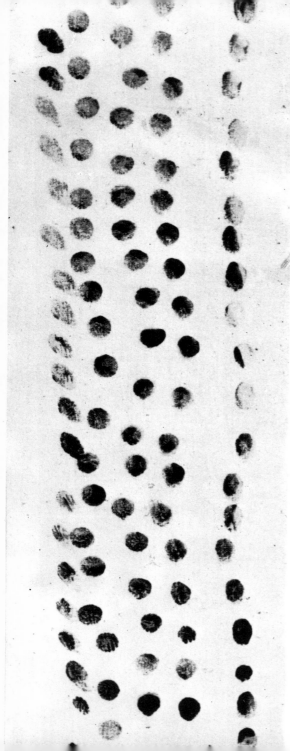

Methods of Work

Finger printing

We are initiated directly into fabric printing if we print with our fingers. The work process, its rhythm, is communicated directly. We find our way freely to arrangements of the given subject matter and sense the effect of working material and tool. In finger printing, the technical aspects of printing may be experienced. We become sensitive to this when it occurs, and to its results.

1

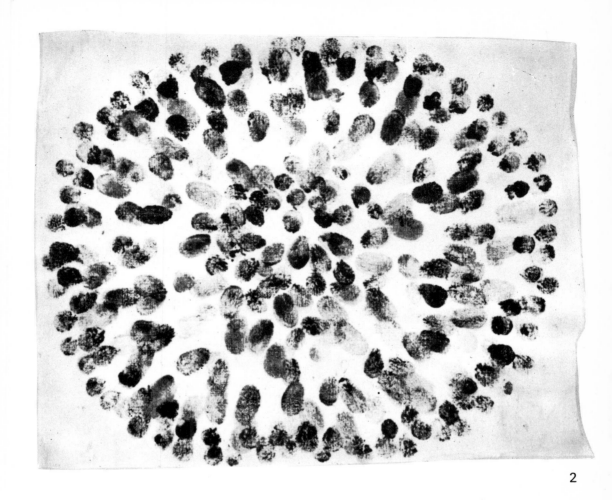

2

Five fingers leave a dynamic trace; the construction of the hand lends itself to the bow-shaped printing motif (1). The radiating form (2) is created when we turn the fabric during printing. The colouration varies between light and dark tones; the amount of pressure used determines the colour intensity.

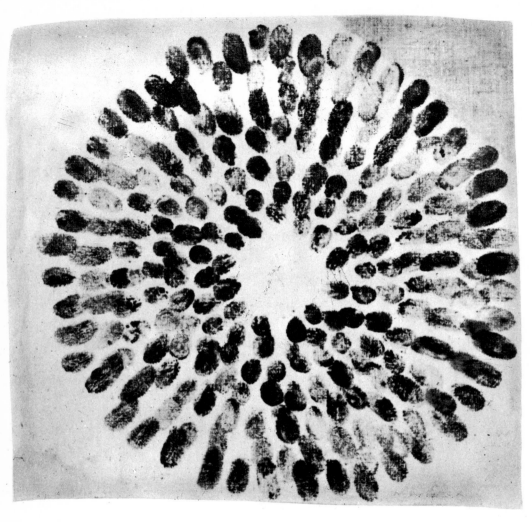

3

In figure 3 an increasing sureness of hand from inside to outside is evident; the rhythm acquired transmits itself to the form. Working with both hands increases the concentration on the printing operations and in the creation of forms one's imagination unfolds.

The more densely and evenly the stamped shapes draw together, the more clearly the spaces between them stand out as negative shapes (8, 9). As they are formed by the positive shapes, we experience these constrasting shapes as belonging to one another. The ranging of these 'pairs of opposites' lends an area the effect of a 'rhythmic unity.' Here we encounter elementary rules of ornamentation (according to Wersin). They are valid for application to any utilitarian item we choose (9).

The cork stamp

Cork is bark tissue of the cork oak. It is light and elastic, but also brittle. Its structure is a factor to be considered in printing and one that lends charm. Because it is difficult to cut cork cleanly, we use the angular and round shapes obtainable commercially (12).

The shapes are limited to squares and circles. Mixtures of colours enliven a simple arrangement (10). If we space out the squares (11), we obtain effective countershapes with the intervening spaces.

Opposite we seek contrast in different sizes of stamps (13).

10

11

12

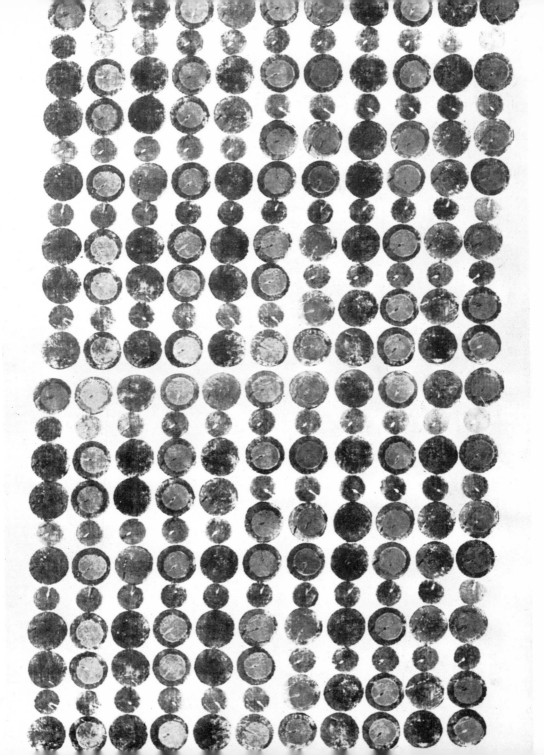

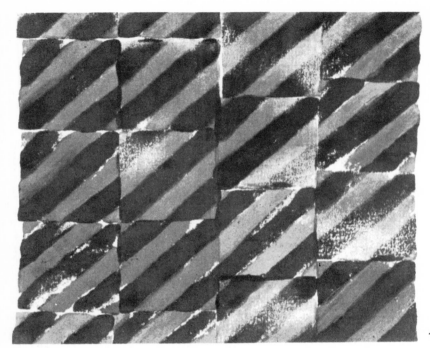

14

15a

15b

15c

16

The felt stamp

It is natural to use inking-pad felt for printing. The material, since it becomes saturated with dye, may be imprinted several times with results of almost the same intensity before it is dipped into dye again (for this purpose poured on a glass plate). Firm and resilient saddler's felt is a suitable material. It is cut out as desired and glued to an appropriate piece of wood. Smooth pieces, cut with a knife, scissors, or a punch, are best in this fibrous working material (15a, b, c).
A simple shape may also be painted on the felt and imprinted (15c). In this case printing with several colours at a time is most attractive (14, 17). The borders between the colours may become slightly blurred but this can be corrected with a fresh application of colour.

17

The permanent ink dyes have a transparent effect; mixed colours appear if different shades are laid one on top of the other (18a, 16). Both ties (18a and b) were printed with the same stamp but, in the case of the left-hand one, the intervening spaces were over-printed in addition.

18a

18b

20

The round boxes above were covered with coloured book cloth and afterwards patterned with opaque permanent colour (20).

With punches of different sizes we can make a set of stamps (15a) that allows us to interchange shapes (19). As felt stamps can be imprinted several times in succession without re-inking they are employed for larger areas of material; the table cloth opposite (19) measures 2 ft. 8 in. × 4 ft.

The clay stamp

Clay can be kneaded into stamps that are easy to handle and rich in form (22, 23, 24); the soft material lends itself to the imagination. After a firing at 1470°–1650°F. (800°–900°C.) the stamps are usable. The porous pot takes up colour well and favours an even imprint.

The printing surfaces here have patterns pressed into them (22, 23, 24). A leather-hard shape can be imprinted in a clay surface so that a negative is obtained on a counter-stamp, as is demonstrated by the doll's dress (25). The negative shape of stamp (24) cannot be fitted into the positive shape in printing. This is only possible with symmetrical shapes (28). Figures 26 and 27 show how stamp 23 can be used.

22

23   24   25

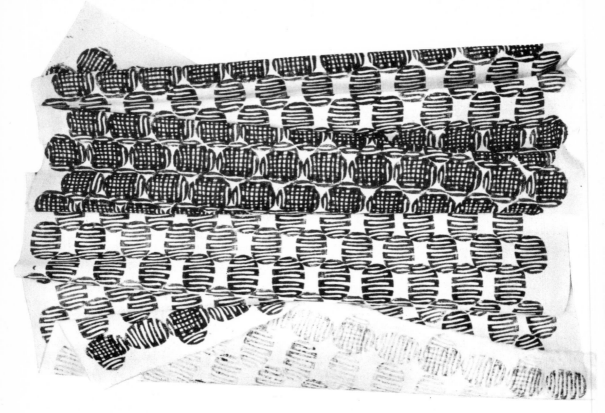

26

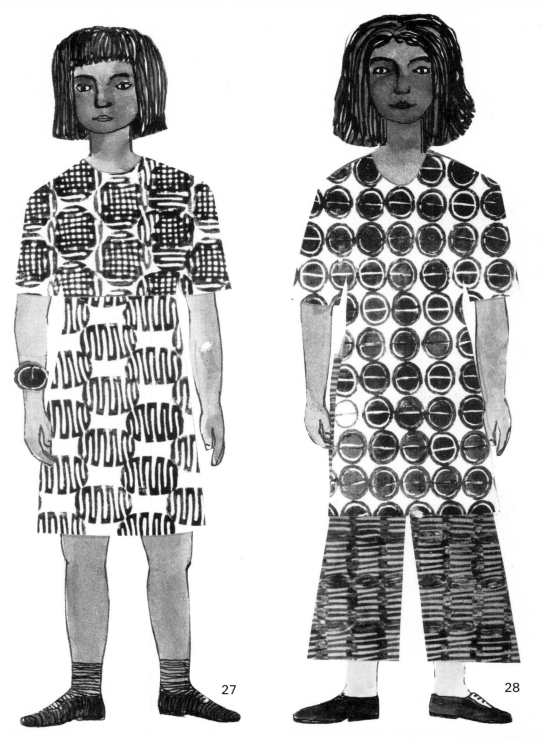

27

28

31

30

Stamp made of wood dowelling

Round and square stamps of dowelling are versatile and stable printing tools. We cut them as desired from dowelling of various thicknesses. Their printing surfaces can be modified even by children, with a file, which is easily manipulated. Here the filed profiles determine the contour of the stamps (30). The circle and the square are both embossed in this way.

By simple means we alter the basic form decisively. When it is printed we recognize the free play we have gained (29, 31).

When used for an object the ornamental arrangement may be adapted to the shape (32). The upright line, decisive directions, and expanses must be considered. Here the sections of cloth, which had been cut out as required, were printed before they were sewn together.

32

34

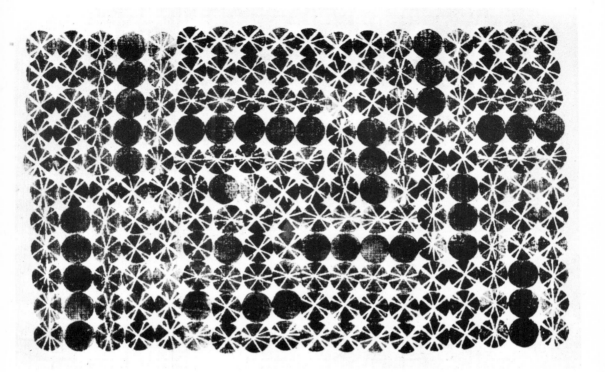

33

The constructed stamp

In printing with a single stamp the question arises of whether one can obtain a result in a quicker way. Identical or similar shapes may be put together into pattern units (34), which we can insert in repeat or in a different direction (33). The technique required is taken into account.

In constructing stamps considerations are based on previous experience. Technical ideas and aims with regard to design complement each other.

34

35

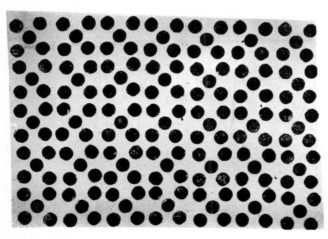

Round rods of equal length were inserted in a piece of wood. An electric boring machine guarantees drill-holes of equal depth if it is appropriately adjusted. The 'plug stamps' (37) were rounded to fit the hand. Pieces cut out for dolls' clothes show how the dotted pattern may be applied (35, 36).

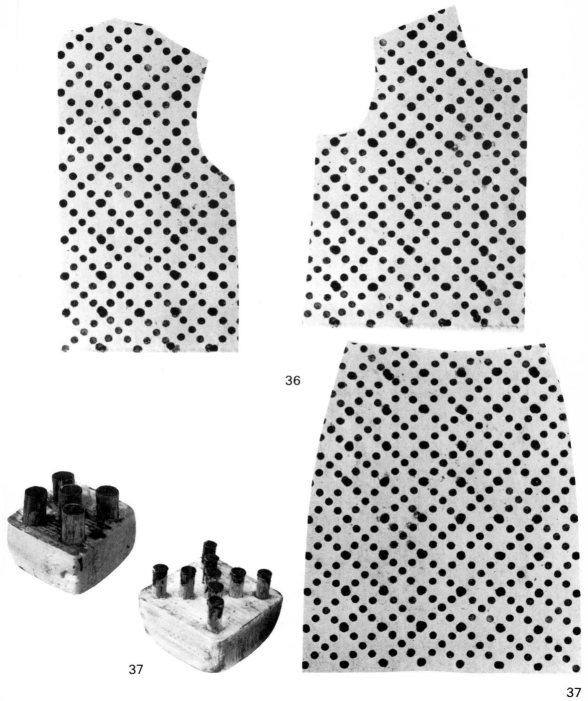

36

37

37

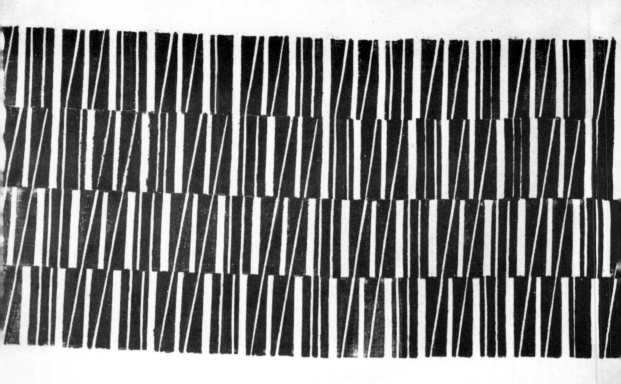

38

39

40

We divide a piece of linoleum (about 3 in. square) by straight or slanting cuts into differently shaped pieces. When it is separated, an alternating series of negative and positive strips is obtained (39). A repeat of such a stamp can be made quite lively if the rows are slightly shifted (38) or colours alternated (43).

Triangular segments were arranged around a centre. This stamp (40) with a diameter of about $5\frac{1}{2}$ in. inspires some splendid work (41).

38

41

42

43

The arrangement of a stamp form (39) in groups of four (42) leads to larger repeat units. In the work below, the wide intervening spaces de- determine the result (43).
The more lively effect of the pointed. shapes opposite (made with artificial leather) is supported by the gradation of colour (44).

45

46

We can make grooves on the surface of linoleum with a linoleum cutting knife. (46). This block may be used for superimposed printing; the imprint is then made denser in dark stripes (45).

42

47

Movable material as a starting point for design

With movable printing material we introduce change, surprise, and chance. Thread fulfils these expectations. For this textile work-material permanent colour is suitable, applied to the stamp with a roller.

We wind a cord around an oblong piece of wood (48). The ends of the cord are gripped in notches and glued. The winding may be shifted; from imprint to imprint new situations arise.

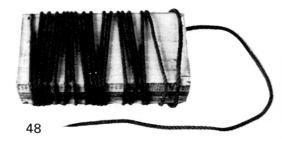

48

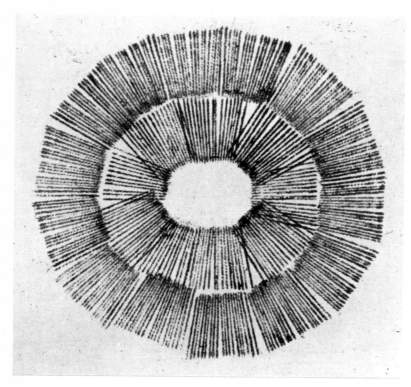

49

We can discern this happening in the ribbon shapes (47). An arrangement around a centre (49) is suggested if we push the strands together on one side. If we imprint the four sides of the stamp by tilting them one after another on to the material we obtain a vertically consistent, linear pattern (51). We can roll the stamp radially from the middle outwards and thus obtain a radiating form (50).

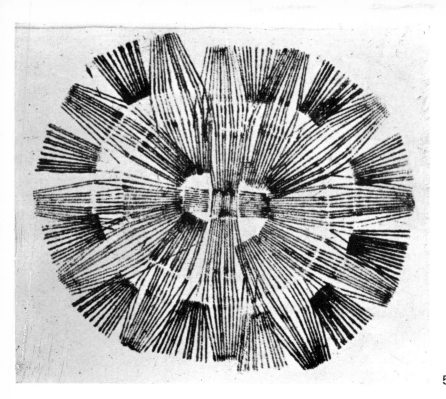

50

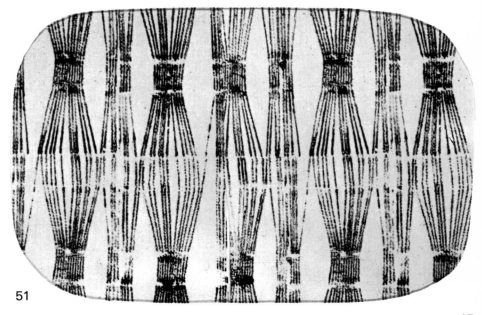

51

45

52

A round piece of wood wound with cord leads to roller printing (52, 53), as described on page 68.

53

54

Thread is ideally suited for spiral and meandering linear forms glued on a block of wood (55, 57). This delicate ornamentation is most effective on fine fabric (56). A multicoloured ground modified the effect of the graphic form (54).

55

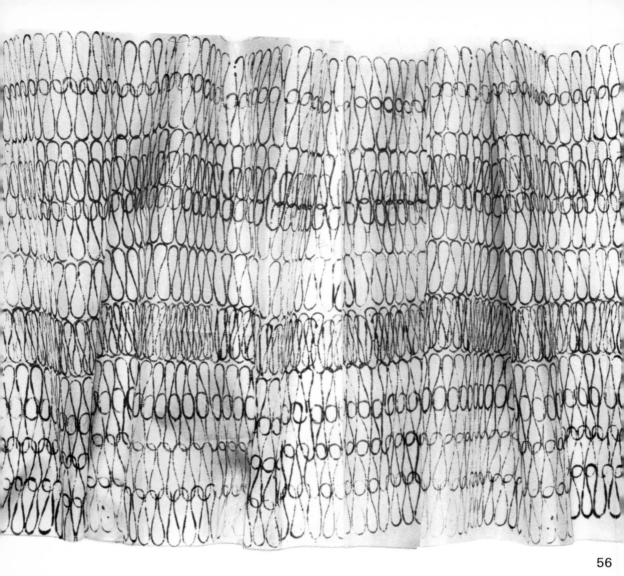

56

48

57

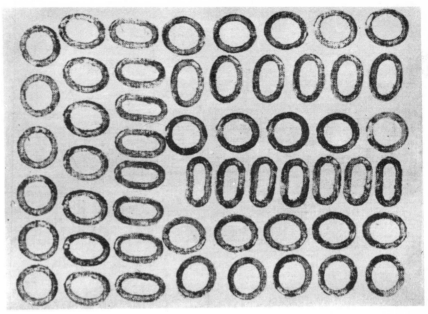

With plastic, we have elastic materials at our disposal: the piece of garden hose (59) makes rings that vary between a circle and an oval under the pressure of the hand (58).

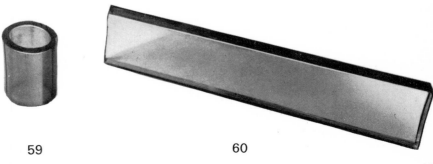

59   60

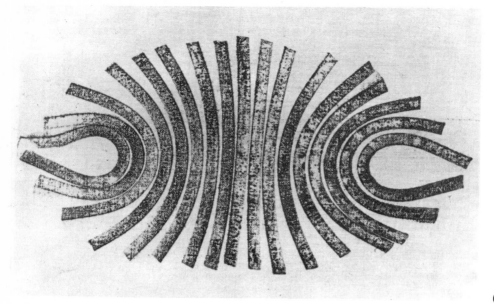

61

62

63

The elasticity of the flexible strip of plastic material (60) can still be discerned in the imprint (61). Plastic material can be reshaped to a limited extent. This fact impels the printer to reflect upon the possible variations of density and arrangement.

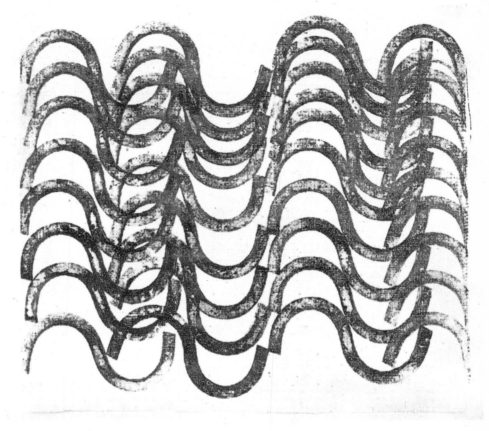

64

We anchor the elasticity when we grip the plastic material in a specially prepared piece of wood (62, 63). These shapes are repeatable (64).

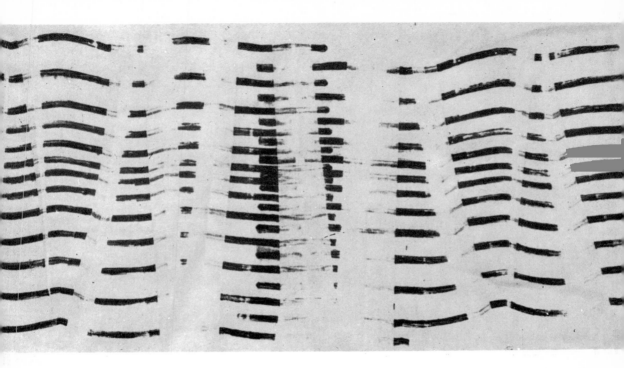

68

The fabric ground, which we generally stretch out smoothly, can also be manipulated. We can place it in folds before printing, and in this way prevent parts of the fabric from receiving the dye (65–68). The striped patterns above and opposite were printed with strips of plastic (67, 68) and wood dowelling (66). The 'fold technique' is also suitable for patterns cut in linoleum (65).

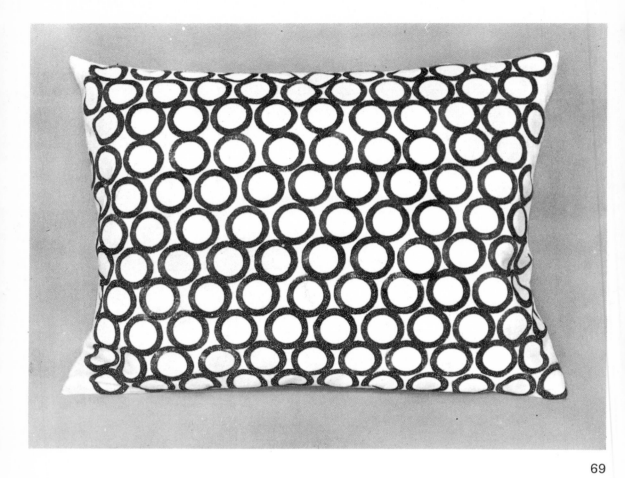

69

Simple multicolour printing

In multicolour printing several printing shapes of different colours complement each other in a total design. This can be accomplished by the negative shapes of the first block appearing as positive ones on the second. In the so-called reprinting process the mirror-image imprint of the positive form, while it is still wet, is imprinted again on the second block so that it can then be worked out in a way that fits in with the positive as a counter-relief.

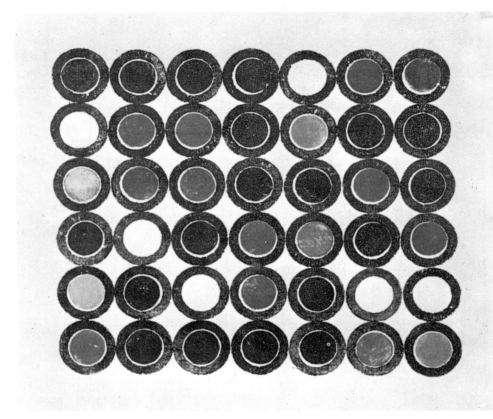

In fabric printing we can get around these difficulties if we select simple contrasting shapes that fit into one another, like rings (69) and circular areas with which we fill in the rings with colour (70).

Symmetrical shapes will complete each other without any reprinting process, as the clay stamp print (28), the rectangles constructed in colours (71, 72), and the circles (70) show.

Plywood letters (73) are composed as both negatives and positives. The fret-saw technique permits the counterforms to join exactly (74).

71

72

73

74

75

The carved block

The stamp used by craftsmen is a block carved out of hard wood. In its advanced form it requires advanced skills. Here we start with basic techniques and simple patterns.

We select a variety of firm wood good for carving, such as apple, pear, or elm. We should avoid, for example, the conifers, which split easily, and the brittle, soft alder, since these may break under strong pressure.

The carving of a piece of wood is subject to certain rules. The block above (75), which was prepared with a sandblast blower, demonstrates the importance of the grain. Here the grain takes on an effective, decorative role (76). However, this wood would not be suitable for carving. For carving we select long wood that has grown evenly (the grain-pattern therefore follows the growth of the trunk). Even here we must take into account the way the wood's fibres run when working on it. Saw, drill, and various chisels are at our disposal. These tools leave different marks according to the purpose for which they are used; we should respect them and develop our ideas of design from familiarity with our tools and with our wood, which is a working material with a will of its own.

Every piece of wood to be carved must be clamped, irrespective of its size. We must use both hands in carving, in order to guide the tool carefully and, at the same time, push it forward powerfully.

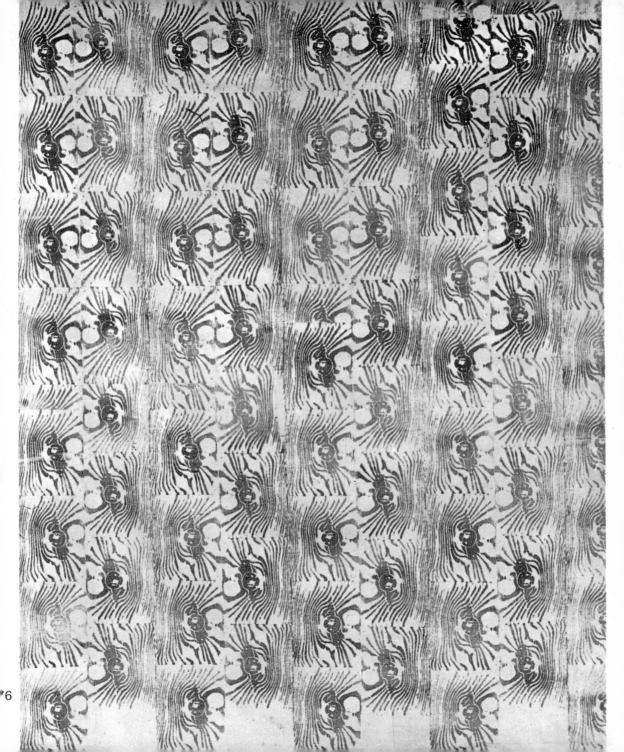

77

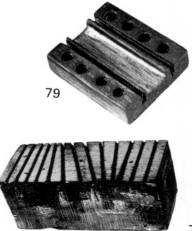

79

78

80

Here a sash saw was used against the grain (78). The sawcuts produce soft lines on the fabric (77). The varying application of colour supports the linear movement. In the case of the wooden stamp (79), the saw served to make the work easier; between the cuts the wood fibres were lifted out cleanly with a chisel. This open stamp shape is supplemented by drill holes. Their possibilities become apparent during printing (80).

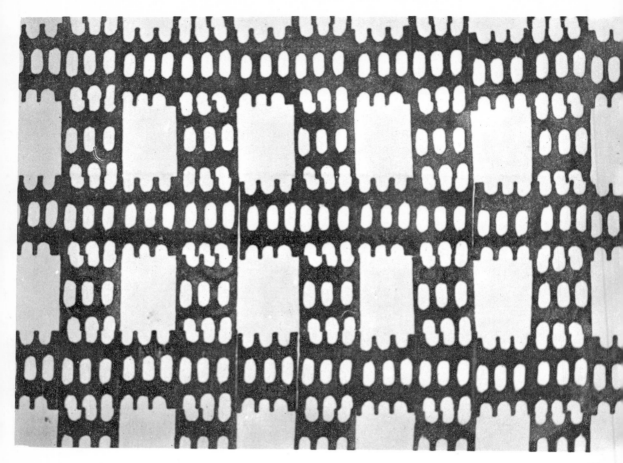

81

62

82　　83　　84

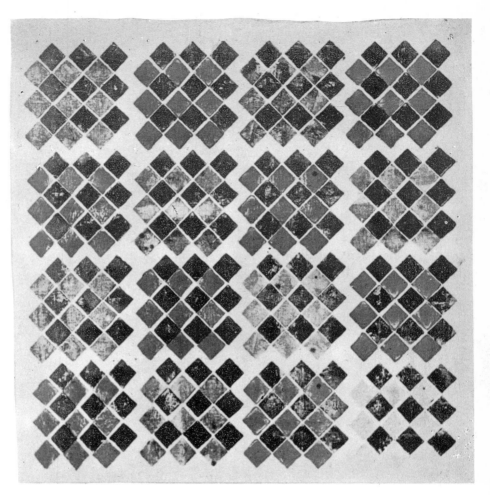

85

86

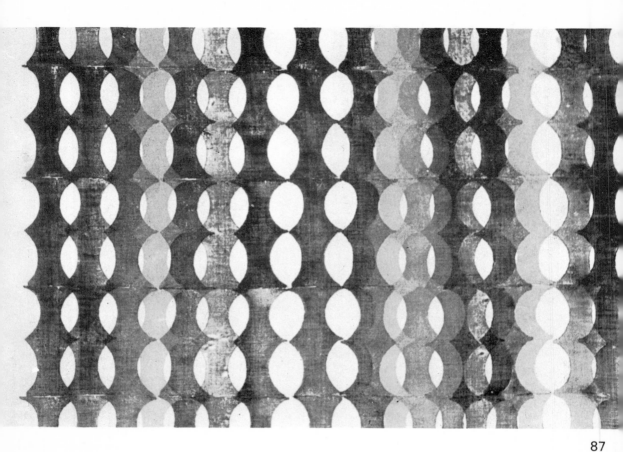

Hollow chisels (83) produce rounded contours. Where the cutting width is from $\frac{3}{4}$–$1\frac{1}{4}$ in. they inspire splendid work. The relation between tool and pattern becomes clear and can be observed in the prints (81–91). Straight-cut edges are achieved with the chisel (84). This is first placed vertically so that its chamfer (the slanted cutting surface) faces the area to be cut out; we pierce the fibres, creating a hollow within which we can now chip away carefully. The printing stamp (86) was developed from the tooling. Its clear shape allows variations in arrangement (85).

With a distinctive carved form (89) we decide immediately on a simple method of printing, the repeat (90).

The rather plain block (88), on the contrary, leaves manifold possibilities of expression open to us (87). For this piece hand-printing colours were applied thinly and printed on batiste, giving a transparent effect.

88

89

90

91

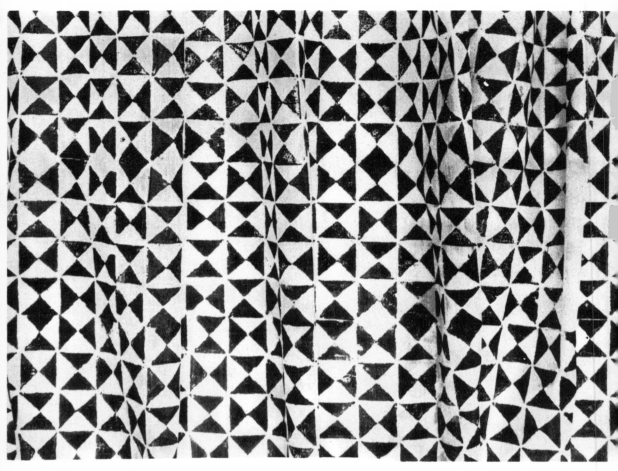

92

93

94

66

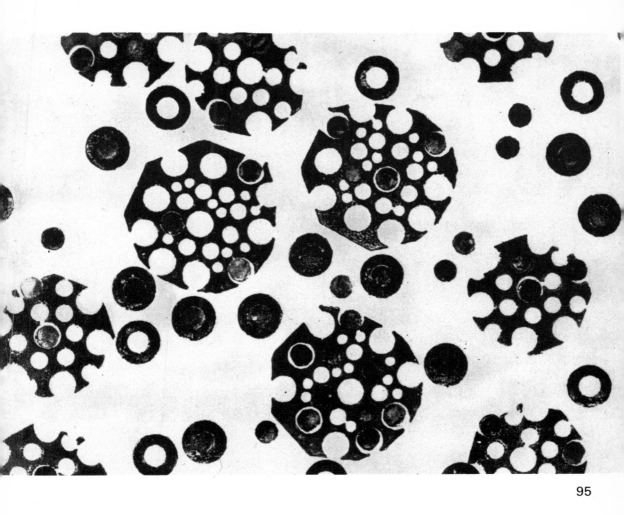

95

The square block (94) is designed for a repeat; it is most effective over large areas (92).
The stamp (93), shaped with a drill and a band saw, demands a looser spacing into which smaller stamps can be introduced to complete it. Multicoloration assists the play of forms (95).

96

Roller printing

One technical difficulty in printing is the even distribution of pressure, which becomes more apparent as the block becomes larger. For this reason a resilient pad underneath is particularly important. With a roller, on the other hand, we can transfer the colour on to the fabric without any trouble. The roller has almost supplanted plate printing in the textile industry. Its advantages are greater clarity and precision in the printing process. We use the linoleum roller for our purposes.

The roller print creates uniform squares that fit together without any perceptible joins (96). This technically-controlled printing tool may be modified to produce a multitude of different shapes (99, 100). Of course, the amount of colour diminishes with each revolution so colour gradations appear. On fine fabrics this is not a disadvantage, as the indistinct borders of areas have a most attractive effect.

For sharp contours we must insert a 'stopper'. We can achieve this most simply by splitting a round wooden roller (97). With this 'cradle' we obtain sharp-edged shapes similar to block printing (96). At the same time we can use this half-roller for gradations within the shapes (98).

97

98

99

100

We can change the wooden roller with saw cuts. With a mitre we cut it at a 45° angle (101). This austere pattern (102) rolls out as a broad, wavy band (104). The surprise here is to see a straight cut turn into a wavy movement. The negative shapes suggest an expansion of the motif (105). For the repeat roller (103) the borders of the pattern were sawn at angles of 45° and 135° and the negative forms removed. The positive and negative forms, which match each other, can also be fitted together. Large areas may be patterned easily and quickly with this roller (105); hand-printing becomes systematic and precise.

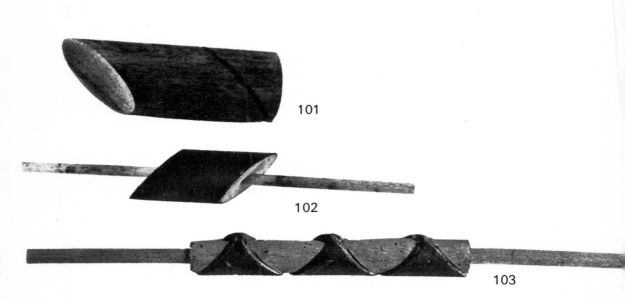

101

102

103

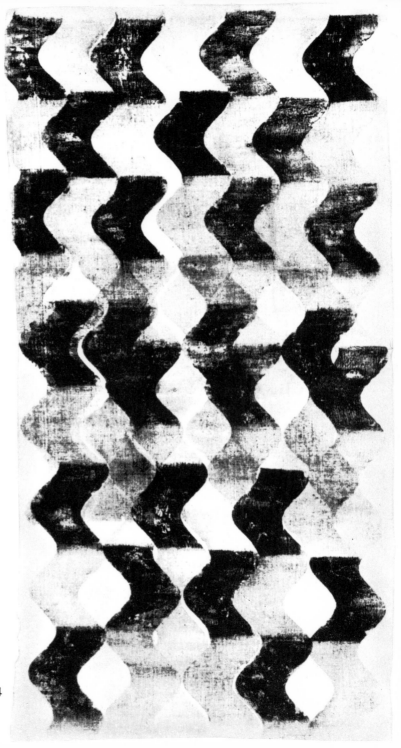

104

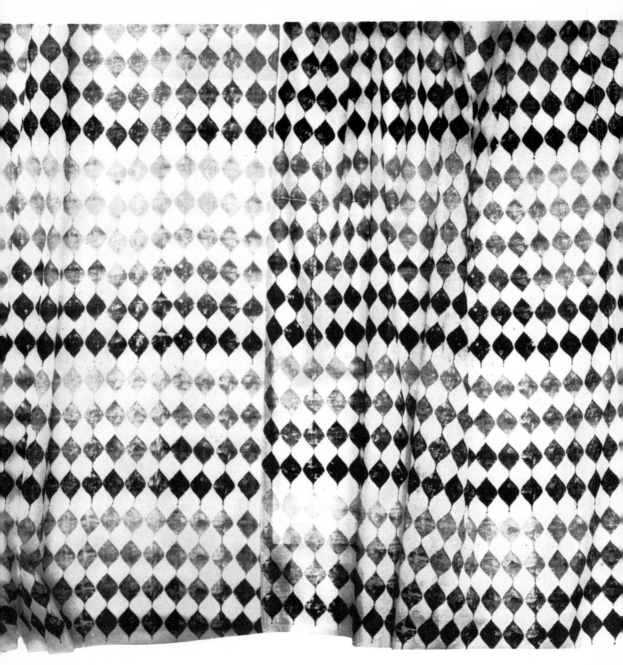

106

The results of the carved printing surface of a roller are not easy to visualize, or predict, from a design on a flat surface. They are created when a printing pattern cut into a curved surface is projected on to a flat surface.

We can, however, place shapes that were conceived flat on the roller by using another material, for example, artificial leather (107) or felt. In cutting the patterns we require we consider the size of the cylinder they are to encompass. The open shape on the roller (107) forms positive and negative diamonds on being printed (106).

107

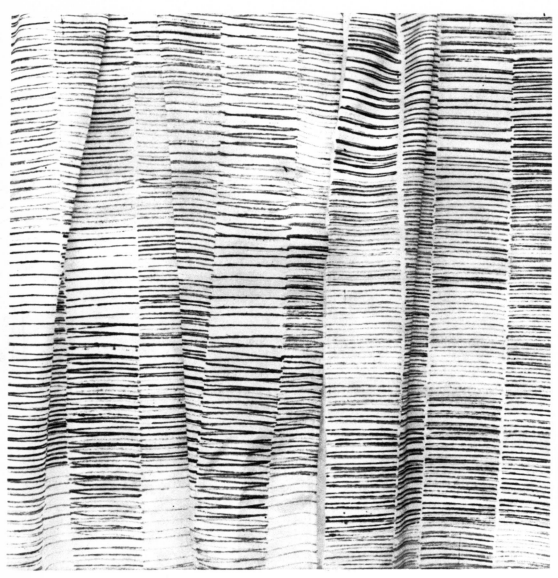

109

Metal is a well tested printing material. Strips of copper, 1/20 in. thick, are clamped into grooves sawn in a roller (110). The fine lines are suitable for printing on lampshade silk (108), natural silk and batiste. Different densities, a check (109), expressed here with a square rod, and multi-coloration, form themes for the use of this kind of roller. Large pieces of fabric hung in folds make simple patterns effective.

110

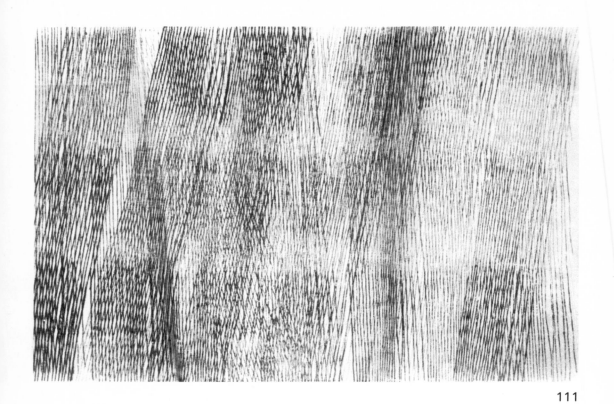

111

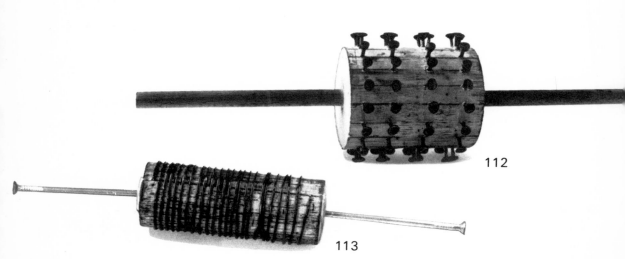

112

113

114

We continue our theme with nail- and wire-rollers (112, 113). Instead of short lines across we have dots (114) or continuous lines (111). The winding of copper wire around the roller corresponds to the winding of cord (53) but it differs from the latter in its sharp printed effect. The ends of the wire must be tightly secured in a special notch or in drill holes.

Experience with metal inspires the introduction of a blueprint block (116). Blueprinting is an old resist printing process in which the fabric was dyed in indigo after the pattern had been printed with a 'paste' that resisted the indigo. The metal pins of the block served to transfer the paste. The process resulted in a white pattern on a blue ground.

However, we are interested here in the direct printing process, and the old patterns prove their worth in reverse (117). We fill in a broadly-spaced pattern, formerly designed to be effective on a dark ground, as we print it in dark on a light background (115).

The old-time ornamentations prove their form valid in this play of patterns, and valid for our day.

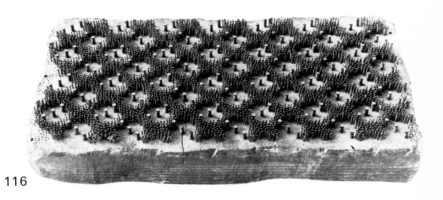

116

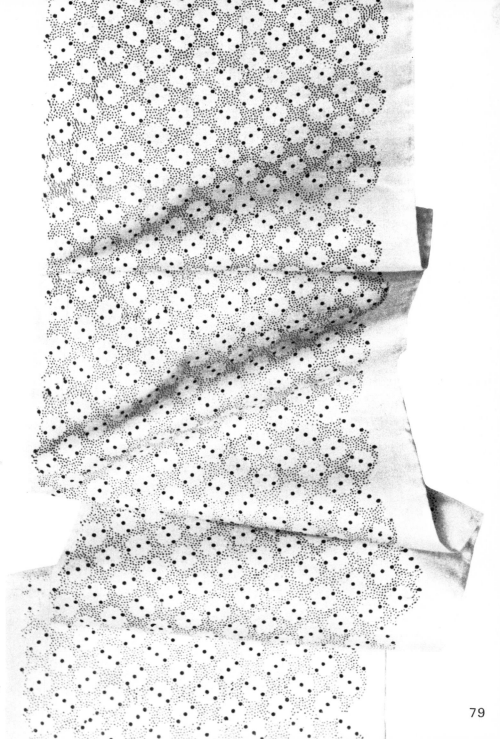